teenagers

Translation: Jean Grasso Fitzpatrick

English translation © copyright 1987 by Barron's
Educational Series, Inc.

© Parramón Ediciones, S.A.
First Edition, April, 1985
The title of the Spanish editions is *Los jóvenes*

All inquiries should be addressed to:
Barron's Educational Series, Inc.
250 Wireless Boulevard
Hauppauge, New York 11788

Library of Congress Catalog Card No. 87-12429

International Standard Book No. 0-8120-3851-7

Library of Congress Cataloging-in-Publication Data

Solé Vendrell, Carme, 1944-
  Teenagers.

  (The Family)   3000300010742
  Translation of: Los jóvenes.
  Summary: A simple explanation of what teenagers are and
their place in the family. Includes a guide for parents and
teachers.
   1. Youth – Juvenile literature. [1. Adolescence.
2. Youth. 3. Family] I. Parramón, José María.
II. Title. III. Series: Family (Barron's Educational
Series, inc.)
HQ796.S581413   1987   305.2'35   87-12429
ISBN 0-8120-3851-7

Legal Deposit: B-1311-88

Printed in Spain by EMSA
Diputación, 116
Barcelona (España)

8   9   9960   9 8 7 6 5 4 3 2

the family

teenagers

Carme Solé Vendrell

J. M. Parramón

BARRON'S
New York • Toronto • Sydney

Teenagers are a lot like you, only taller...

and stronger...

and braver.

They like to have fun with their friends ...

and dance up a storm ...

and play sports …

and study together…

and go to school together.

But sometimes they feel lonely, and worried, and sad.

Sometimes when a boy meets a girl …

they fall in love.

Do you have a big brother or sister?
Or a babysitter who goes to high school?

They're teenagers!

TEENAGERS

Adolescence is a time of enormous changes, and the years from 13 to 20 are among life's most intense. This is the time when children ask themselves, "Who am I? What do I want out of life?"

A new, different body

Teenagers are not only bigger than young children, their bodies are more adultlike. Teenage boys' voices deepen and their beards begin to sprout; teenage girls' breasts begin to grow. Sometimes teenagers seem to be all gangly arms and legs, but soon they can walk, run, jump, and swim better than ever. After all, the Olympic gymnast Nadia Comaneci and the tennis player John McEnroe both won championships at the age of sixteen!

Gradually, a boy becomes a man and a girl becomes a woman. Their bodies are ready to have children, but usually they will not be married until they are older. Meanwhile, they will be growing up in mind and spirit, and will need plenty of understanding from those around them.

Friends

We all have friends, but teenagers seem to need them more than anybody. Teenage friends dress alike, listen to the same music, and compare notes on their parents and teachers.

First love

Teenagers are very emotional, and first love can be very romantic and intense, with many ups and downs.

A new view of the world

The teenage years are a time to analyze and discuss the world. Young children will accept their parent's ideas, but teenagers develop their own point of view.

Love, work, and independence

Some teenagers get in trouble at school, or become depressed, or involved with drugs and alcohol. Loving parents and other adults can help them solve these problems. Getting a job or developing a new interest can be a positive way of achieving the identity and independence necessary for a teenager to become a successful adult.

The teenage years are between twelve or thirteen and nineteen or twenty. This period, which leads to young adulthood, is often considered the most tumultuous time of human life.